Did Y

EAST YO

A MISCELLANY

Compiled by Julia Skinner

With particular reference to the work of Maureen Anderson,
Clive Hardy, John Markham, John Milnes, Robert Preedy,
Roly Smith and Graham Wilkinson.

THE FRANCIS FRITH COLLECTION

www.francisfrith.com

First published in the United Kingdom in 2010 by The Francis Frith Collection®

This edition published exclusively for Identity Books in 2010 ISBN 978-1-84589-535-8

British Library Cataloguing in Publication Data

Did You Know? East Yorkshire - A Miscellany
Compiled by Julia Skinner
With particular reference to the work of Maureen Anderson, Clive Hardy, John Markham,
John Milnes, Robert Preedy, Roly Smith and Graham Wilkinson.

The Francis Frith Collection
Frith's Barn, Teffont,
Salisbury, Wiltshire SP3 5QP
Tel: +44 (0) 1722 716 376
Email: info@francisfrith.co.uk
www.francisfrith.com

Printed and bound in Malaysia

Front Cover: **FLAMBOROUGH, HEAD, NORTH LANDING 1886** 18001p

The colour-tinting is for illustrative purposes only, and is not intended to be historically accurate

CONTENTS

INTRODUCTION

The landscape of East Yorkshire is a walker's paradise. Rich and fertile farmland swells gently from the flat, fertile meadows of Holderness, and gradually rises and rolls over the chalky uplands of the Yorkshire Wolds, to end with a flourish at the Flamborough Headland. The Humber estuary and the North Sea mark its southern and eastern boundaries. The economy of the area is mainly based on agriculture and tourism to the region's long coastline, but there is much of interest to the visitor apart from the seaside, including historic buildings, nature reserves and the Wolds Way long distance footpath, running 79 miles from Hessle to Filey on the coast, just over the East Yorkshire border.

The Wolds area is rich in archaeological remains, with a profusion of Neolithic, Bronze Age and Romano-British sites. It is one of the best areas in Britain for studying the archaeology of the Neolithic period; there are more than 1,400 Bronze Age round barrows (burial mounds) on the Wolds, many of which are still prominent features in the landscape; and there are Roman villa sites at Rudston, Harpham, Brantingham, Welton and Rudston, where the Rudston Monolith can be found – dating from the Neolithic period, it is the largest standing stone in England. In the south of the region the Southern Wolds lie between the plain of Holderness to the east and the Vale of York to the west. This is an agricultural area with many attractive villages, such as Walkington, Bishop Burton and Skidby. The market towns of Pocklington and Market Weighton are sited between the Central Wolds and the Vale of York, whilst the scarp of the Western Wolds swings northwards from Garrowby Hill to Ganton in North Yorkshire. Great Driffield (usually known as just Driffield) is 'the capital of the Wolds', although Kilham formerly had this role.

Hull is the largest settlement in East Yorkshire and the third largest port in Britain, with docks running for several miles along the north bank of the Humber through which hundreds of millions of pounds worth of cargo and thousands of passengers pass every year. The county town of East Yorkshire is Beverley, built around its historic Minster. Bridlington is the largest of the seaside resorts along East Yorkshire's long coastline, which runs from Spurn Point at the southern end to the dramatic chalk cliffs of the Flamborough Headland at the north, a designated Heritage Coast

ULROME, THE CHURCH c1960 U34050

EAST YORKSHIRE DIALECT WORDS AND PHRASES

'Appen' – perhaps.

'Balling' – crying.

'Booling' – pushing a pram or bike.

'Bray' – to hit, beat or break.

'Dowly' – miserable damp or dreary weather.

'Fendable' – capable.

'Fettle' – to clean something, or to put it in good order.

'Fuzzock' – a donkey.

'Kecks' – trousers.

'Larkin' – playing, messing about.

'Lop' – a flea.

'Mafting', hot, as in **'it's mafting'** – the weather's really hot.

'Menseful' – neat, decent, orderly. **'It will mense it off'** – it will finish it off nicely.

'Nesh' – cold, as in cold weather. **'I'm neshed'** – I'm really cold.

'Putten aboot' – harassed, very busy.

'Rackets' – a local word from Beverley for small lanes and alleys that link streets.

'Stagnated' or 'fair capp'd' – greatly surprised.

'Stall'd' – fed up with, wearied or tired of something.

'Taffled' – tangled.

'Worrawolly' – a simpleton, fool.

Did You Know?

EAST YORKSHIRE

A MISCELLANY

BRIDLINGTON, MEN ON THE QUAY c1885 18042x

HAUNTED EAST YORKSHIRE

Skipsea is said to be haunted by the ghost of the niece of William the Conqueror. She was the wife of Drogo de Bruerer, a Flemish knight who took part in the Norman Conquest of England of 1066, for which he was rewarded with the hand of the royal niece in marriage and the estate of Skipsea, where he built a now-lost castle. The marriage was not a success: Drogo fed his wife poison, claiming that it was a love potion, then fled to the continent before his evil deed was discovered. The ghost of his murdered wife is said to haunt Castle Hill at Skipsea to this day.

Burton Agnes Hall near Bridlington is said to be guarded by the spirit of Anne Griffith, one of the daughters of Sir Henry Griffith who had the present house built between 1598 and 1610 (see photograph 18021, page 31). Anne was very excited about the building of the new house, but was attacked by robbers and mortally injured shortly before it was completed. Before she died, she asked her sisters to have her head cut off after her death and preserve it in the Hall so that her spirit could watch over the house and the family; her wishes were ignored and she was buried in the churchyard, but her ghost created such a disturbance at the Hall that her sisters had to agree to her body being exhumed and her wishes being carried out. The Hall remained undisturbed by her spirit as long as her skull was not removed from the building, so eventually it was bricked into a wall of the Hall and remains there to this day.

A ghost story linked with Flamborough tells how a local girl in the past called Jenny Gallows committed suicide by throwing herself into a chalk pit, and her restless shade haunts the area. If children playing nearby disturb her spirit, they can protect themselves from her by reciting the following rhyme:

> *"Ah'll tee on me bonnet*
> *An' put on me shoe,*
> *An' if tho's not off*
> *Ah'll suan catch thoo."*

The Bull and Sun pub in Bridlington is probably the town's most famous haunted pub, but another local pub linked with mysterious activity is the Londesborough: a barrel was found moved in the cellar when no one was there, and there have also been several sightings of a mysterious man sitting in a corner of the function room.

The Sun Inn at Beverley is said to be haunted by ghostly Dominican monks from the nearby former friary in Friar's Lane, who died when a tunnel connecting the friary to the pub collapsed whilst they were inside. The old friary, now a Youth Hostel, is itself said to be haunted by a ghostly old man who makes noises and is disruptive, particularly active in Room 2. Sightings of ghostly friars have also been reported in the kitchen and the dining room, unexplained footsteps have been heard, and a strange white apparition has been seen moving along the top floor of the building.

One of Beverley's most famous ghost stories is that of Sir Josceline Percy, whose headless spectre is said to drive a phantom coach-and-four around the streets of the town. Another local story, recorded in 'A Glossary of Words used in Holderness' (1877), was that the ghost of a prisoner who committed suicide was believed to haunt the Beverley Borough Gaol. He was known as 'Awd Simmon Beeather' because of the work, called beating simmon, which the prisoners did – this involved beating, or pounding, brick or tiles into a powder ('simmon') used by bricklayers for colouring mortar. However, the Borough Gaol in Beverley was only used for the confinement of persons committed for trial, or who had received light sentences; prisoners sentenced to hard labour such as beating simmon were confined in the House of Correction for the East Riding, also in Beverley, so perhaps that was really the building linked with the ghost story.

Ye Olde White Harte Inn in Hull is the subject of several mysterious occurrences. Visitors have reported a strange sensation of being watched, particularly in the Functions Room on the second floor, where some customers have complained of being touched, kissed or hit by something invisible, and glasses and bottles have been seen moving across the table, pushed by an unseen hand. There have also been sighting of glowing orbs, and a strange, shimmering shape in the gents' toilet. A skeleton of a woman, apparently murdered, was found in one of the walls of the pub and her skull, affectionately known as Freda, is kept behind the bar.

EAST YORKSHIRE MISCELLANY

Beverley originated as a religious centre around a monastery founded in the eighth century by John, the retired Bishop of York, who was canonised as St John of Beverley in 1037. Reports of miracles wrought through St John of Beverley's intercession brought many pilgrims to Beverley to visit the shrine which held his remains, causing the town to grow and prosper. In the Middle Ages Beverley was also a centre of the textile industry, known for high-quality cloth; the town had strong trading links with the cloth towns of the Low Countries, and many Flemish weavers and merchants came to live in Beverley – they are recalled in the street name of Flemingate, which means 'the street of the Flemings'. Beverley's Market Cross in Saturday Market, built in the early 18th century, is a symbol of the town (see photograph 45284, below, and photograph B80078 on page 51). It is sometimes still called the Butter Cross after the farmers' wives who traditionally sold their dairy goods nearby.

BEVERLEY, MARKET PLACE 1900 45284

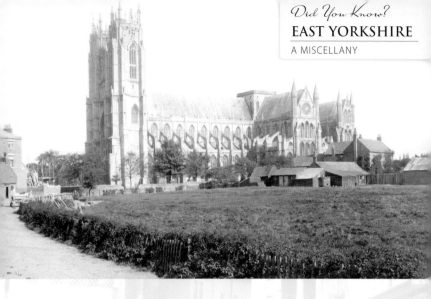

BEVERLEY, THE MINSTER, SOUTH WEST 1894 34778

A rebuilding programme of Beverley Minster from the 13th to
the 15th centuries produced the great church seen today. The
magnificent structure is, however, dedicated to St John the Evangelist,
not St John of Beverley. Beverley Minster is one of Europe's most
beautiful and finest churches. The Early English east end was begun
in 1220 (see photograph 17875, page 47), and the magnificent
Perpendicular west front was completed in 1420. One of the
glories of the minster is the canopied Percy Tomb next to the High
Altar, one of the finest examples of 'decorated' medieval funerary
ornamentation. It is probably the tomb of Lady Eleanor Percy who
died in 1328, but it may be that of Lady Idonea Percy who died in
1365. In the 14th and 15th centuries the aristocratic Percy family lived
at Leconfield Castle, north of Beverley.

Dominican friars (the 'Black Friars') arrived in Beverley in 1240; they were popular preachers and attracted a strong following, with Beverlonians leaving bequests to their friary rather than to one of the town's churches. The resulting antagonism of the Minster clergy to the friars is given visual proof in a carving in one of the Minster's misericords (small wooden benches), showing a fox in a friar's habit preaching to geese, which represent those residents of Beverley foolish enough to listen.

Photograph 17887 (opposite) shows the superb west front of St Mary's Church in Beverley. The famous Minstrels Pillar in this church is a colourful reminder of the town's long connection with minstrelsy – in the Middle Ages Beverley was where minstrels from the north of England gathered for their annual meeting. The capital of the Minstrels Pillar is carved with a group of five musicians (although most of their instruments were damaged during the Civil War), and is believed to have been a monument given by the Northern Guild of Musicians when the church was rebuilt in the 1520s. Minstrelsy is also commemorated in a carving on a wooden misericord in Beverley Minster, where a sow is shown standing on her hind legs as she plays a set of bagpipes, whilst her four piglets dance to the music.

The East Riding House of Correction opened in Beverley in 1810 and closed in 1878. A famous inmate was Robert Peddie, the leader of the Chartist rising in Bradford in 1840. He was incarcerated here from 1840-43, and recorded his unhappy experiences in a series of verses, 'The Dungeon Harp'.

William Crosskill, born in Beverley in 1799 and mayor of the town in 1848, has been called 'the father of mechanised farming in East Yorkshire'. He had an iron foundry off Mill Lane which made iron work for public utilities and agricultural machinery and equipment. His most notable invention was the 'Clod Crusher', a disc harrow with side teeth for cultivating the soil of ploughed land ready for sowing, which won him a Gold Medal from the Royal Agricultural Society.

**BEVERLEY, ST MARY'S CHURCH,
WEST FRONT c1885** 17887

BEVERLEY, NORTH BAR WITHOUT 1894 34796

Beverley was protected in the Middle Ages by four gates, known as 'bars'. The North Bar is the only one that survives, and is shown in photograph 34796, above. In past years Yorkshire Motor Services had specially designed buses made with a curved 'Gothic-style' roof so that a driver could negotiate his way under the low and narrow archway. The buildings close to North Bar Without in this photograph, No 4 (in the middle) and Nos 6-8 (far left of the photograph), were given a Victorian medieval-style facelift by Beverley carver James E Elwell, who incorporated carvings of their earlier appearance into the decoration of Nos 6-8, and also cartoons of the 19th-century Prime Ministers Benjamin Disraeli and William Ewart Gladstone.

In the chancel of All Saints' Church at Bishop Burton near Beverley is a chalice brass to Peter Johnson, a 15th-century vicar of the parish, which is one of the earliest examples of this kind of brass work. There is also a bust of John Wesley, founder of the Methodist movement, which was carved from an elm that grew on the green where he preached. The local pub has the unusual name of the Altisadora – it was named after a racehorse which won the St Leger in the 19th century.

The town of Market Weighton was famous as the home of William Bradley, believed to have been the tallest man ever to have been born in Britain. He was born in 1787, and grew to be 7 feet 9 inches tall. He travelled the country as 'the Yorkshire Giant' before retiring to Market Weighton, where he died in 1820. A plaque outside his house in York Street shows the size of the shoes he used to wear, and he is remembered in his home town with an event known as 'Giant Bradley Day' each year. The extra-large chair which he used can still be seen in the Londesbrough Arms in the town.

MARKET WEIGHTON, HIGH STREET c1960   M178032

WARTER, COTTAGES AND WAR MEMORIAL c1955 W320003

Photograph W320003 (above) shows the picturesque thatched cottages behind the war memorial in the pretty village of Warter, near Pocklington. The church of St James in Warter, completed in 1864 in 14th-century style, is no longer used for worship; it is now a heritage, entertainment and educational resource called the Yorkshire Heritage Centre which is under the control of the Yorkshire Wolds Buildings Preservation Trust, formed in 1996 to save the church from demolition.

The town of Pocklington is believed to have been the scene of the last witch-burning in England in 1630, when a mob of local people hauled 'Old Wife Green' to the market place and burned her to death before they could be stopped – by this date it was customary to execute a 'witch' by hanging, rather than burning, which was the fate of Petronel Haxley, wife of a local blacksmith, who was accused of witchcraft and hanged in Pocklington's market place in 1642. The town was the scene of another tragic death in April 1733 when the showman Thomas Pelling, 'The Flying Man', tried to fly from the tower of the parish church using a pair of home-made wings; he was killed when he collided with a buttress and a plaque on the church records that he was buried 'exactly under the place where he died'. The event is recalled in the town's annual Flying Man Festival, a weekend themed around aerial and flying activities.

Work began on Howden's beautiful minster church of St Peter and St Paul in the early 13th century, but the project was not completed until the 15th century (see photograph H274008, below). In the Middle Ages Howden became a place of pilgrimage as a result of miraculous tales linked with 'John of Howden', an early canon of the minster known for his piety and humility, who died in 1275; it was said that his corpse raised its arms from his open coffin during his funeral, as if to greet the host. John of Howden has never been recognised as a saint by the Catholic Church, but the income which Howden Minster received from the pilgrims who came here to his shrine fulfilled John's prophecy that he would continue to aid the minster after his death – during his lifetime he had been responsible for the rebuilding of the minster's choir.

HOWDEN, THE CHURCH c1955 H274008

Goole's development began in the early 1600s, when the Dutch engineer Cornelius Vermuyden was brought in to construct the 'Dutch River' of the River Don, diverting it northwards to the Ouse to drain the marshland of Hatfield Chase in South Yorkshire. (He is commemorated in the name of the Vermuyden School in Boothferry Road.) The town grew around the confluence of the 'Dutch River' with the Ouse where it flows into the Humber. The first settlement was on the eastern side of what is now known as the Dutch River Bridge, an area now known as Old Goole. 'New Goole', or what is now known as Goole, grew up on the other side of the river when the port was developed by the Aire and Calder Navigation Company in the 1820s, linking Goole via their canal from Knottingley; this allowed coal to be brought from the West Yorkshire coalfield for transfer to seagoing vessels at Goole; the 'Dutch River' had made the lower River Don navigable for barges from the South Yorkshire coalfields to do the same. The first building in 'New Goole' is believed to have been the Lowther Hotel on Aire Street, which has recently been restored, and now houses residential, office and retail accommodation. Goole celebrated its centenary in 1926 with the erection of a clock tower in the town centre, seen in photograph G157023, below.

GOOLE, MARKET CENTRE c1955 G157023

GOOLE, THE DOCKS c1955 GI57015

Goole's small but busy port handles nearly 3 million tonnes of cargo each year, but is located so far inland from the sea that it has been called a 'port in green fields'. Historically the commodity most handled by the post was coal, but pit props were also imported through Goole, and were stored floating in the water at the 'Timber Pond'. The decline in the coal mining industry put an end to this part of the port's business, and the former Timber Pond is now used as a marina.

Henry VIII's religious changes of the 1530s provoked bitter opposition in many parts of the country, but nowhere more so than in the north of England, where a rebellion took place in 1536 called the Pilgrimage of Grace. The leader was Robert Aske, a Howdenshire lawyer. Howden Minster (see page 15)became the centre of the rebellion, and its processional cross was used as the rebel banner; the cross disappeared during the conflict, and has never been found. The rebellion was unsuccessful, and Robert Aske was executed. Howden Minster survived Henry VIII's Dissolution of the 1530s, but later fell into ruin. Part of the minster has now been restored – the nave, central tower and transepts – and serves as the parish church for present-day Howden, whilst the east end remains ruinous and is in the care of English Heritage.

COTTINGHAM, HALLGATE c1955
C344012

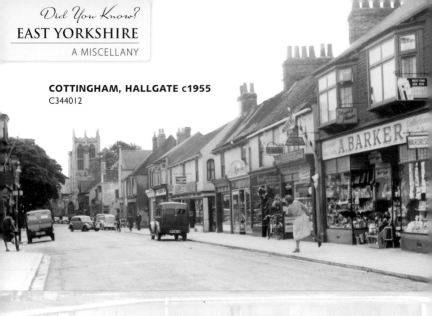

West of Hull is the village of Cottingham. A licence from King John in 1200 granted the right to hold a market, fairs and to fortify nearby Baynard Castle, which remained the manor house of Cottingham until the 16th century when it burnt down; only the mound on which it was built survives, surrounded by a substantial moat on four sides. In the background of photograph C344012 (above) the tower of Cottingham's Gothic-style parish church of St Mary can be seen; inside the church are some notable monuments to the Burton family of Hotham (which held land around Cottingham in the 17th century), and some tombstones with monumental brasses dating from the late 14th century.

The municipal cemetery in Cottingham is where the famous novelist and poet Philip Larkin is buried. Larkin lived in the area whilst working as the chief librarian of the Brynmor Jones Library at Hull University, a role he undertook for 30 years from 1955 until his death in 1985.

Brough-on-Humber's development took off when The Blackburn Aircraft Company opened its first factory here in 1916. It mainly manufactured naval and maritime aircraft – one well known type was the Blackburn Beverley, used by the RAF as a heavy lift transport between 1955 and 1967. The town is famous for its links with the 18th-century highwayman Dick Turpin, who regularly stayed at the Ferry Inn on Station Road under the alias of John Palmer, and was arrested there under that name in 1738 for causing a fracas in the street and threatening behaviour. He was taken to the House of Correction in Beverley, but as he was also suspected of horse-theft

he was transferred to York Castle to be tried at the Assizes. It was there that his true identity was discovered, and he was tried for his many crimes, including murder. He spent his final days in the condemned cell of York's prison before being hanged. His grave is in St George's churchyard in York.

Yorkshire's last working windmill is at Skidby. Built in 1821, the four-storey tower mill had four sails, each weighing 1.25 tons. The mill has now been restored, and is preserved, together with its neighbouring warehouses, as the Museum of East Riding Rural Life. Wholemeal flour is produced at the mill on its working days for sale in the mill shop.

The Humber Bridge connects East Yorkshire with Lincolnshire, and carries around 120,000 vehicles per week. When the bridge was opened in 1981 it was the largest single-span suspension bridge in the world, at 4,626ft long. The total length of wire in the cables of the bridge is 44,000 miles – more than 1½ times the circumference of the Earth.

The Humber-side town of Hessle is now a suburb of Hull, but it dates from a settlement in Anglo-Saxon times called 'Hoesellea', meaning 'the hazel grove'. Hessle's parish church of All Saints was completely rebuilt in the 12th century, and despite much rebuilding in the 18th and 19th centuries, some stonework at the west end of the nave from this time. The western tower of the church, with its graceful spire, was erected in the 15th century; it was used as a landmark by shipping in the Humber, and apparently also served as target practice at some time in the past – during restoration work in 2008, a bullethole was discovered in the weathercock on the top of the spire.

HESSLE, PRESTONGATE c1955 H467308

The Humber Bridge Country Park near Hessle is formed from an old chalk quarry – chalk quarrying was a major local industry in the past. The old Black Mill on Hessle Foreshore was used to grind boulders of chalk into whiting, which was carried away by Humber boats to be exported all over the world. The Phoenix Sculpture Trail through the park features 10 sculptural seats whose design was inspired by the reserve's historical heritage.

A common sight on the Rivers Hull and Humber in the past were Humber keel boats, with their distinctive ketch-rigged sails. Despite their cumbersome appearance, these boats carried up to fifty tonnes of cargo, were extremely manoeuvrable, could sail close to the wind, and could be handled by one man. Their origins are obscure, but their rig suggests a direct descent from the Viking trading vessels that once plied the Humber, Ouse, Don and Trent.

In the first quarter of the 19th century Hull was the biggest whaling port in Britain. Hull men sailed the northern waters around Greenland and Spitsbergen in search of whales, at that time a valuable source of oil for use in lamps and as a lubricant. Sailors occupied themselves on the long voyages by carving intricate designs on whales' teeth or walrus tusks and then highlighted the design by rubbing lampblack or ink into the incised lines. There are examples of these carvings, known as scrimshaw, in the Town Docks Museum in Hull. After whale fishery came to an end in the 1860s, Hull became the world's largest centre for oil seed crushing and milling; this led to the establishment of many industries such as paint, colour, oil and varnish manufacture.

On the corner of Boulevard and Hessel Road in Hull stands the Fishermen's Memorial, a statue of George Smith, skipper of the Hull trawler 'Crane', who was killed during an incident known as 'The Russian Outrage' which occurred in 1904. Russia was at war with Japan, and in the early hours of 22 October 1904 the Russian fleet opened fire on a group of Hull trawlers fishing on the Dogger Bank, mistaking them for Japanese torpedo boats.

HULL, THE HUMBER 1903 49820

Hull (properly Kingston upon Hull) is on the north side of the River Humber where it is joined by the River Hull. Hull began in the 12th century as a hamlet named Wyke upon Hull. It was acquired by Edward I in 1293 as a supply base for his campaign against the Scots, re-named Kingstown (later Kingston) upon Hull, and became one of the foremost ports of the realm. Hull's first dock was constructed in 1778, and more docks were to follow during the 19th century. However, bomb damage

during the Second World War and redevelopment has changed much of Hull's dockland heritage. The former Queen's Dock was filled during the 1930s and the area is now Queen's Gardens; the Humber Dock and Railway Dock have been converted into a thriving marina; and the Prince's Dock, whilst still containing a large expanse of water, is now one of the principal shopping areas following redevelopment during the 1980s and early 1990s.

The imposing Dock Offices seen in photograph 49806 (below) are evidence of Hull's status as a major port. Hull's situation on the east side of the country meant that most of its trade was conducted with the Scandinavian countries, the Baltic States, the Hanseatic ports and the low countries of Europe. The centre of its merchant trade was conducted in High Street, formerly known as Hull Street, which followed the line of the river; the merchants built many substantial and richly-adorned houses along its frontage adjoining their staithes, or private wharves. The names of the merchants who built these houses or were associated with them are reflected in the superb examples that survive today: Blaydes House, the Maister House, Crowle House and Wilberforce House.

HULL, DOCK OFFICES 1903 49806

Hull was fortified in the 14th century with massive protective walls and five principal gates which gave entry and exit to the city. Hull was regarded as a strategic prize by both the Royalists and the Parliamentarians during the Civil War, and local historians will tell you that the war began in Hull when, on 23 April 1642, Charles I was refused entry to the city through the Beverley Gate, at the west end of Whitefriargate; this was the first action of defiance against the king of the Civil War. It was in a room now known as the 'Plotting Parlour' in Ye Olde White Harte Inn (then the Governor's home) that the Governor and other leading citizens decided to follow Parliament's instructions and refuse to let the king enter Hull and take control of the arsenal that was stored in the city.

HULL, GEORGE STREET 1903 49814

Photograph 49814 (above) of George Street in Hull in 1903 shows the statue of the poet Andrew Marvell in its original position. Andrew Marvell was born in March 1621 in the nearby village of Winestead. As well as being a great poet, he was also MP for Hull for 20 years, a friend of John Milton and an admirer of Oliver Cromwell. The statue of Marvell now stands in front of Holy Trinity Church.

The statue of King William III in Roman classical style in Hull's Market Place is shown in photograph 49813x, opposite, known locally as 'King Billy'. Local folklore says that when the king hears the clock of the nearby Holy Trinity Church strike midnight, he dismounts and avails himself of a drink in the nearby King William Hotel!

The area of East Yorkshire along its coastline is known as Holderness. It is low lying, flat, fertile land, which was marshland until it was drained in the Middle Ages. The Holderness coastline suffers the highest rate of coastal erosion in Europe, with an average 1.5 metres (5 feet) of coastal land being lost to the North Sea each year.

Seven miles to the east of Hull is the Holderness village of Paull. When Charles I was blockading Hull during the Civil War, a military battery was built here. This position was later used in the Napoleonic Wars, and again in the Second World War as an anti-aircraft gunnery post. Now Fort Paull, restored in 2000, is an absorbing war museum.

HULL, MARKET PLACE 1903 49813x

**WITHERNSEA,
THE LIGHTHOUSE
c1960** W1770310

In 1669 Henry Guy presented The Great Mace to the Holderness town of Hedon to celebrate his election to Parliament as the town's MP; it is claimed to be the oldest civic mace (a ceremonial staff) in the country. Hedon is also famous for its magnificent church of St Augustine (dedicated to St Augustine of Hippo), a Grade I listed building over 800 years old which is recognised as one of the architecturally-best three churches in the north of England. Its 130ft tower is a landmark for miles around. St Augustine's Church at Hedon is known as the 'King of Holderness'; the 'Queen of Holderness' is St Patrick's Church at Patrington, a masterpiece of the Decorated period with a graceful, lofty spire which rises to 189ft and is a prominent landmark across the flat fields. Sir John Betjeman wrote that the church 'sails like a galleon of stone over the wide, flat expanse of Holderness'.

Spurn Point (also known as Spurn Head) is a sand spit at the southern end of East Yorkshire's coastline, reaching out into the North Sea. It is a designated National Nature Reserve, important as a feeding ground for wading birds. The Humber Lifeboat is based at the southernmost point of Spurn Head. In December 1978 the lifeboat crew under coxswain Brian Bevan carried out what has been described as one of the most daring and skilful rescues in the history of the RNLI to save the five-man crew of the stricken freighter 'REVI'. They had to bring the lifeboat alongside the 'REVI' 35 times in a fierce storm with towering seas, a mission so dangerous that the entire crew were awarded for gallantry.

The builders of Withernsea lighthouse (W1770310 opposite) were conscious of the severe erosion suffered on the Holderness coast when they constructed it in 1894, for they built the soaring tower several hundred yards inland, in the middle of residential streets. It is now a museum, partly dedicated to Kay Kendall, a famous film star of the 1950s who was born in the town. Her family were much involved with maritime life in Withernsea, and her grandfather, Robert Drewery, worked on the construction of the lighthouse; he was also the coxswain on the last rowing off-shore lifeboat from 1911-1913. The base of the lighthouse displays many exhibits relating to the RNLI and HM Coastguard, including ships' bells, models and old photographs recording the history of shipwrecks along this coast, as well as a special display that commemorates the Withernsea lifeboats and crews.

GREAT DRIFFIELD, MIDDLE STREET SOUTH c1955 G35000I

Great Driffield – usually known as just Driffield – is 'the capital of the Wolds'. There are several local customs linked with the new year: on New Year's Eve people gather in the market place to hear the church bells ringing in the new year, and in the first few days of the new year local children take part in 'scrambling', when they walk through the town calling out a traditional rhyme and are given sweets, money and other gifts by shopkeepers. Driffield was the home and workplace in the 19th century of Benjamin Fawcett, one of England's finest woodblock colour printers, assisted by the artist Alexander Francis Lydon. He is most famous for his long association with Francis Orpen Morris, an eminent ornithologist and entymologist; Morris wrote a number of famous books on natural history which were printed at Fawcett's printing premises in Middle Street in Driffield, featuring engravings of illustrations by Lydon.

Aldbrough is one of the largest of the Holderness coastal villages. There was once a moated castle nearby that belonged to the de Melsa family, which died out in 1377. The village church of St Bartholomew (built 1377) has two tombs and effigies believed to be of the last of the de Melsas. One of the tombs is of Sir John de Melsa, who was Governor of York from 1292 to 1296 and also a renowned warrior.

Burton Agnes Hall near Driffield is a fine late Elizabethan stately home still owned by the descendants of Sir Henry Griffith who designed and built it (see photograph 18021 below). The Hall is open to the public and contains superb carvings and plaster work, fine alabaster chimney pieces and a large collection of English and French paintings.

BURTON AGNES, THE HALL c1885 18021

The name of Hornsea, midway between Flamborough Head and Spurn Point, means 'the horn shaped lake', a reference to the large freshwater lake in the area known as the Mere. Many old houses in Hornsea were built of stones and pebbles, as was the church of St Nicholas, built of cobblestones in the 14th century. Hornsea was once the home of the famous Hornsea Pottery, founded in 1949, which closed in 2000. The Hornsea Museum has a permanent exhibition of Hornsea Pottery, with over 2,000 items on display.

Sewerby Hall was built between 1714 and 1720 (photograph 18019, below), and the estate was bought by Bridlington Corporation and opened to the public in 1936. The Hall now houses the Museum of East Yorkshire with displays of local history and archaeology and the Coastguard Museum, as well as beautiful period rooms.

SEWERBY, THE HALL c1885 18019

SLEDMERE, THE MONUMENT c1960 S401001

Sledmere House near Driffield has been the home of the Sykes family since the 18th century. The monument shown in photograph S401001 (above) stands opposite Sledmere House. Erected in 1919, it commemorates the Wagoners Reserve Corps of 1,127 local farm workers who joined Sir Mark Sykes's private army as wagon drivers in the First World War. The Wagoners Museum in Sledmere House chronicles their story.

BRIDLINGTON, ADMIRING THE VIEW 1913 66248v

The chalk cliff of Flamborough Head juts out over Bridlington Bay, giving Bridlington itself some protection from the fierce northerly winds. The town was originally divided into two parts: the Quay, where the fishermen lived in their cottages, and the 'old town' one mile inland, centred around Bridington Priory, where in 1119 Walter de Grant founded an Augustinian priory. A 14th-century prior was later canonised as St John of Bridlington, patron saint of local fishermen and women in difficult labour, after whom St John Street in the town is named.

Bridlington Priory became wealthy and important in medieval times, but in 1536 the last prior took part in the northern rebellion against Henry VIII known as the Pilgrimage of Grace and was executed. After the rebellion King Henry dissolved the priory, but its nave became Bridlington's parish church of St Mary, shown in photograph 74295, below. On the right of the photograph is the medieval Bayle Gate, originally the priory gatehouse; it has been used at various times over the centuries as a courtroom, barracks, a prison and a school, and is now the Bayle Gate Museum.

BRIDLINGTON, PRIORY CHURCH AND BAYLE GATE 1923 74295

BRIDLINGTON, NEW SPA 1903 50015

The first hotel was built in Bridlington in 1805, but the town took off as a popular holiday resort with the arrival of the railway here from Hull in 1846; new buildings sprang up between the Old Town and the Quay, and the two parts of the town were linked together. The present 'Brid', as it is fondly known, has two piers, both built in the 19th century.

Many a vessel has come to grief while trying to round Flamborough Head to the safe harbour of Bridlington. The lighthouse at Flamborough (photograph 59914, page 41) was designed by Samuel Watts and built by John Matson of Bridlington and was first lit in December 1806. The last lighthouse keepers left in 1996, when Flamborough Lighthouse was automated.

BRIDLINGTON, SS YORKSHIREMAN 1932 B206179

This photograph shows the excursion ship SS 'Yorkshireman' in Bridlington's harbour in 1932. In May 1928, this vessel started service in Bridlington, and except for the war years she spent every summer at the town. She could carry up to 400 passengers on her sea excursions. During the winter she did towing work on the Humber. She was finally towed to Belgium in 1954 and was broken up in 1965.

In 1779 the peace of the East Yorkshire coastline was shattered by the noise of gunfire when the ships of the Royal Navy and the ships of the American Continental Navy Squadron led by John Paul Jones came together in the battle of Flamborough Head, one of the most famous naval actions of the American War of Independence. The name 'Flamborough' is Norse, and means 'settlement on a headland'. The villagers of Flamborough made their living mainly from the sea in the past, but if a local fisherman was baiting his line, he would think it unlucky if a fox, hare, rabbit or pig were mentioned, and would abandon his fishing for that day.

A huge earthwork runs across the Flamborough headland from the nature reserve on the southern side near Sewerby to Cat Nab on the north. It is known as Danes Dyke, but it was probably constructed much earlier than the Viking period, by Iron Age people. The massive ditch and bank earthwork was probably constructed as a defensive measure, with the rampart topped with a wooden palisade.

FLAMBOROUGH, HEAD, NORTH LANDING 1886   18001

Did You Know?
EAST YORKSHIRE
A MISCELLANY

**FLAMBOROUGH,
THE LIGHTHOUSE
1908** 59914

BRIDLINGTON, HARBOUR 1913 66246

SPORTING EAST YORKSHIRE

Claimed to be the oldest horseracing flat race in England, the annual Kipling Cotes Derby is held near Market Weighton each March. The race dates from 1519 and is run over a 4-mile course over farm lanes and tracks. Each rider pays an entrance fee, and the money thus raised is given to the rider who comes second, whilst the winner receives the interest on a sum of money that was invested back in 1618 – consequently, the rider who comes second often receives more prize money than the actual winner!

Horse-racing has been an important feature of Beverley for over 300 years. Originally it took place on the Westwood and with the erection in 1768 of the first stand on the northern section – the Hurn – it became one of the attractions of the Georgian town. New grandstands were built in 1959 and 1967. The peace of the Westwood at Beverley was disturbed in the past by such violent activities as the rule-less, large-scale annual football matches that were played on the Sunday before the races, but these were banned by the town's magistrates in 1825.

Hull City Football Club was originally based at a site on the north side of the Anlaby Road. The club moved to a new ground on the Boothferry Road in 1847, and has now moved to a brand new state of the art stadium near to its original site on the Anlaby Road, which is shared with Hull FC (Rugby League). A record attendance at a Division Three game was set at Boothferry Park on Christmas Day 1948, when 49,655 people attended a game against Rotherham. Hull City's David Mercer played every single game played by the club during the First World War, part of a run of 218 consecutive appearances for the Tigers.

Probably the most famous sportsman to have come from Beverley is football goalkeeper Paul Robinson, who has played for the England team more than 40 times. Paul Robinson was born in the town in 1979. Beverley was also the birthplace, in 1986, of one of Britain's top tennis players, Katie Jill O'Brien, a former British No 1, who has won four ITF singles titles and two ITF doubles titles.

Hull FC (Rugby League) has the dubious distinction of having lost more major finals than any other club, including three successive challenge Cup Finals between 1908 and 1920. Here are two rather better records: Hull FC's Lee Jackson holds the record for the fastest ever try in a professional game. Playing against Sheffield Eagles at the Don Valley Stadium in 1992, he scored after just nine seconds. In the 1978/79 season in Division Two, Hull FC won every game, the only time this has been achieved in professional Rugby League. Another local Rugby League club is Hull Kingston Rovers; when the club moved to the 'new' Craven Park for the 1989/90 season, the main stand had a unique feature: it was built with 8 hospitality boxes, and was the first Rugby League ground in England to feature such a facility.

Bridlington Rugby Football Club was formed in 1924 from old boys from Bridlington School. The club moved to its current home at Dukes Park in the 1950s; initially there was no clubhouse, and the bath and changing room area were known as the Decontamination Unit! A famous name in the club's history is that of Ernie Cooper, whose name is still in the Guinness Book of Records for the longest goal kick in a game.

Bridlington Town AFC began life in 1918 as Bridlington Central United, and reformed in 1994 under the condition the name was changed to Bridlington Town AFC. The club's nickname is 'The Seasiders'. The club had a notable season in 1992-93, finishing as champions of the NPL Division One, and winning the FA Vase at Wembley. The end of the 2002-03 season also saw the fans celebrate, as The Seasiders won the Northern Counties East League championship 20 points ahead of the runners up, gaining them promotion to the Unibond League.

QUIZ QUESTIONS

Answers on page 52.

1. What is the link between Beverley and Lewis Carroll's classic children's book 'Alice's Adventures in Wonderland'?

2. Why does a beaver feature on the coat of arms of Beverley Town Council?

3. Burnby Hall Gardens at Pocklington are where you will find the United Kingdom's national collection of which plants?

4. Who holds the title of 'Admiral of the Humber'?

5. What in the past were known as 'Tom Puddings', which were particularly associated with the port at Goole?

6. In former times it was a tradition in Stamford Bridge to eat 'spear pies' – what were these, and what did they commemorate?

7. Which man from East Yorkshire was voted the 'Greatest Ever Yorkshireman' in 2000?

8. What did it mean if you became a 'Frithman' in Beverley in the past?

9. Which fictional traveller embarked from the port of Hull on the sea voyage which resulted in him fending for himself for many years on a desert island?

10. Which famous name in aviation history was born in Hull in 1903?

BEVERLEY, MINSTER EAST END c1885 17875

RECIPE

NORTH SEA FISHERMAN'S PIE

In former years a fish pie was the traditional dish in many parts of Yorkshire to be eaten at Easter, on Good Friday.

Yorkshire fishermen have ventured out for centuries from small fishing villages like Flamborough, larger harbours such as Bridlington and the great port and fishing centre of Hull. In its day, Hull was the great fishing port of the British Empire, and was once the home of the world's largest deep-water fishing fleet. Hull trawlers fished the North Sea, the White Sea, and the fringes of the Arctic, particularly for cod. St Andrew's Dock in Hull (see photograph H133037, opposite) was named after the patron saint of fishermen; it was opened in 1883 and handed over for the exclusive use of Hull's 420 fishing smacks. St Andrew's Dock closed in 1975, and the site has now been redeveloped as the St Andrew's Quay leisure and retail complex; hardly any trace remains now of Hull's once great fishing tradition.

For the filling:
350ml/12 fl oz milk
1 bay leaf
Half an onion, finely sliced
450g/1 lb haddock or cod fillet
225g/8oz smoked haddock
  fillet
3 hard-boiled eggs, chopped
25g/1oz butter or margarine
25g/1oz plain flour
75g/3oz shelled prawns
2 tablespoonfuls chopped
  fresh parsley
Lemon juice to taste

For the topping:
500g /1¼ lbs potatoes, cooked
40g/1½ oz butter
60ml/ 4 tablespoonfuls milk
115g/4oz grated hard cheese
  of choice
Salt and pepper

Place the milk, the bay leaf and sliced onion in a saucepan over a medium heat and add the fish. Cover, and poach the fish lightly for 10 minutes. Strain, discard the bay leaf and reserve the milk for the sauce. Flake the fish into a buttered pie dish, discarding the skin and any remaining bones. Add the chopped eggs to the fish.

Melt 25g/1oz butter in a saucepan on a low heat, stir in the flour and cook gently for 1 minute, stirring continually. Remove the pan from the heat and stir in the reserved milk that the fish was poached in, a little at a time and stirring continually so that no lumps are formed. When all the milk has been mixed in, return the pan to the heat and bring the mixture to the boil, stirring continually as the sauce thickens, then simmer the sauce for about 4 minutes, still stirring all the time. Remove from the heat and stir in the prawns.
Add the parsley, lemon juice and seasoning to taste. Pour the sauce over the fish and eggs in the pie dish, and gently mix it all together.

Pre-heat the oven to 180°C/350°F/Gas Mark 4. Gently heat 40g/1½ oz butter in 60ml/ 4 tablespoonfuls of milk in a small saucepan until the butter melts, then add the milk and melted butter to the cooked potatoes, mash and then beat until smooth. Spoon over the fish pie mixture to cover, then score the surface with a fork. Sprinkle the grated cheese over the pie before baking. Bake the pie in the pre-heated oven for 25-30 minutes, until the top is golden.

HULL, ST ANDREW'S DOCK c1955 H133037

RECIPE

GINGER SPONGE PUDDING

At the bottom of Whitefriargate in the centre of Hull Old Town is one of the most intriguingly-named streets in England – Land of Green Ginger. It was formerly known as Old Beverley Street. There are several theories as to how the street got this name, but John Markwell in 'Streets of Hull' explains that this was the part of town where green, or unripe, ginger used to be stored. This sponge pudding also makes a delicious soft gingerbread when eaten cold.

> 175g/6oz self-raising flour
> 75g/3oz caster sugar
> 1 heaped teaspoonful ground ginger
> 50ml/2fl oz milk
> 75g/3oz margarine
> 1 good tablespoonful of golden syrup
> 1 teaspoonful bicarbonate of soda
> A little extra golden syrup to finish

Pre-heat the oven to 160°C/325°F/Gas Mark 3.

Mix the flour, sugar and ginger together. Put the milk, margarine and syrup into a large saucepan, and bring to the boil. Sir well, until the margarine and syrup have melted. Remove the pan from the heat and stir in the bicarbonate of soda. Add the flour, sugar and ginger to the milk and syrup mixture, and mix it all well together. Turn the mixture into a well-greased cake tin 20cm (8inch) square, and bake just above the centre of the pre-heated oven for 30 minutes until the top is firm and golden.

Just before serving, warm a little extra golden syrup in a saucepan and pour over the pudding. Serve hot, with custard or cream.

BEVERLEY, MARKET CROSS c1960 B80078

QUIZ ANSWERS

1. Inside St Mary's Church in Beverley is a carved stone figure of a rabbit known as 'the pilgrim rabbit' because it is dressed in human clothes and carries a medieval pilgrim's bag. Lewis Carroll, author of 'Alice's Adventures in Wonderland', spent time visiting friends in Beverley, and it is believed that this figure inspired him to create either the White Rabbit which Alice follows down a burrow into Wonderland or the Mad March Hare which joined Alice at the Mad Hatter's tea party. The carving may also have been used as a model by Sir John Tenniel for his illustration of either the Mad March Hare or the White Rabbit in the original edition of the book.

2. The name 'Beverley' probably derives from the Anglo-Saxon words 'beofor' and 'leah', which means 'a beaver clearing in the forest'. This is why a beaver features on the arms of Beverley Town Council.

3. The lakes at Burnby Hall Gardens at Pocklington are home to the United Kingdom's national collection of hardy water lilies, actually the largest such collection in Europe.

4. The title of 'Admiral of the Humber' is held by the Lord Mayor of Hull.

5. In the past, coal was carried from Yorkshire coal mines down the Aire and Calder Navigation to the port at Goole in vessels called 'Tom Puddings', short containers that could be coupled together in any length and then towed by barges. When they reached the port of their destination, they were lifted with a hoist and turned upside down so that the coal could be emptied out – just like a pudding being turned out from a pudding bowl.

6. Stamford Bridge was the scene in September 1066 of a battle between the Anglo-Saxon forces of Harold Godwinson, King of England, and a Viking force under Harold Hardrada of Norway. The English were victorious, but there is a local tradition that their advance was held up by a giant Viking axe-man standing on the bridge over the River Derwent; eventually he was killed when an English warrior floated under the bridge in a barrel and thrust his spear up through the planks of the bridge. This led to a local custom in Stamford Bridge of commemorating the anniversary of the battle

by eating 'spear pies' made in the shape of a boat, a tradition which lasted to the early years of the 20th century.

7. William Wilberforce, born in Hull in 1759 and elected MP for Hull at the age of 21, was named the 'Greatest Ever Yorkshireman' in a BBC poll in 2000. He is best remembered for his long campaign against slavery which resulted in the passing of a parliamentary bill to end the slave trade. The tall column on the right of photograph 49806 (page 24) is Hull's monument to him – the first stone was laid on 1 August 1834, the date when slavery in the British Colonies became illegal. The monument is seen here in its original position but it was moved to Queen's Gardens in 1935. The house in Hull (at 23-25 High Street) where Wilberforce was born is now the Wilberforce House Museum, and contains an extensive collection of artefacts relating to the slave trade.

8. The term 'Frithman' was linked with the right of sanctuary which fugitives could claim in Beverley Minster for 30 days. At the end of the sanctuary period they could take the options either of going on trial for their crimes, or banishment abroad, or – unique to Beverley – of becoming a 'Frithman'. If they chose the latter, they agreed to surrender all their property to the Church, become a lifelong servant of the Church, and live in the town for the rest of their lives, albeit penniless, following their previous trades. The word 'Frith' (or 'Frid') comes from an Anglo-Saxon word for 'peace'.

9. Robinson Crusoe, in the book of the same name by Daniel Defoe.

10. Hull was the birthplace of the pioneering aviator Amy Johnson (1903-1941), who became a national heroine as the first female pilot to fly solo from Britain to Australia, at the age of 26, in 1930. She began the historic flight from Croydon Airfield on 5 May 1930. She landed at Port Darwin in Australia nineteen days later, after flying 9,960 miles on a dangerous and eventful trip. She is commemorated in Hull by a statue in Prospect Street. There is also a room dedicated to Amy Johnson at Sewerby Hall, near Bridlington; after her death in 1941, her father gave her memorabilia to the Hall.

FRANCIS FRITH

PIONEER VICTORIAN PHOTOGRAPHER

Francis Frith, founder of the world-famous photographic archive, was a complex and multi-talented man. A devout Quaker and a highly successful Victorian businessman, he was philosophical by nature and pioneering in outlook. By 1855 he had already established a wholesale grocery business in Liverpool, and sold it for the astonishing sum of £200,000, which is the equivalent today of over £15,000,000. Now in his thirties, and captivated by the new science of photography, Frith set out on a series of pioneering journeys up the Nile and to the Near East.

INTRIGUE AND EXPLORATION

He was the first photographer to venture beyond the sixth cataract of the Nile. Africa was still the mysterious 'Dark Continent', and Stanley and Livingstone's historic meeting was a decade into the future. The conditions for picture taking confound belief. He laboured for hours in his wicker dark-room in the sweltering heat of the desert, while the volatile chemicals fizzed dangerously in their trays. Back in London he exhibited his photographs and was 'rapturously cheered' by members of the Royal Society. His reputation as a photographer was made overnight.

VENTURE OF A LIFE-TIME

By the 1870s the railways had threaded their way across the country, and Bank Holidays and half-day Saturdays had been made obligatory by Act of Parliament. All of a sudden the working man and his family were able to enjoy days out, take holidays, and see a little more of the world.

With typical business acumen, Francis Frith foresaw that these new tourists would enjoy having souvenirs to commemorate their days out. For the next thirty years he travelled the country by train and by pony and trap, producing fine photographs of seaside resorts and beauty spots that were keenly bought by millions of Victorians. These prints were painstakingly pasted into family albums and pored over during the dark nights of winter, rekindling precious memories of summer excursions. Frith's studio was soon supplying retail shops all over the country, and by 1890 F Frith & Co had become the greatest specialist photographic publishing company in the world, with over 2,000 sales outlets, and pioneered the picture postcard.

FRANCIS FRITH'S LEGACY

Francis Frith had died in 1898 at his villa in Cannes, his great project still growing. By 1970 the archive he created contained over a third of a million pictures showing 7,000 British towns and villages.

Frith's legacy to us today is of immense significance and value, for the magnificent archive of evocative photographs he created provides a unique record of change in the cities, towns and villages throughout Britain over a century and more. Frith and his fellow studio photographers revisited locations many times down the years to update their views, compiling for us an enthralling and colourful pageant of British life and character.

We are fortunate that Frith was dedicated to recording the minutiae of everyday life. For it is this sheer wealth of visual data, the painstaking chronicle of changes in dress, transport, street layouts, buildings, housing and landscape that captivates us so much today, offering us a powerful link with the past and with the lives of our ancestors.

Computers have now made it possible for Frith's many thousands of images to be accessed almost instantly. The archive offers every one of us an opportunity to examine the places where we and our families have lived and worked down the years. Its images, depicting our shared past, are now bringing pleasure and enlightenment to millions around the world a century and more after his death.

For further information visit: www.francisfrith.com

INTERIOR DECORATION

Frith's photographs can be seen framed and as giant wall murals in thousands of pubs, restaurants, hotels, banks, retail stores and other public buildings throughout Britain. These provide interesting and attractive décor, generating strong local interest and acting as a powerful reminder of gentler days in our increasingly busy and frenetic world.

FRITH PRODUCTS

All Frith photographs are available as prints and posters in a variety of different sizes and styles. In the UK we also offer a range of other gift and stationery products illustrated with Frith photographs, although many of these are not available for delivery outside the UK – see our web site for more information on the products available for delivery in your country.

THE INTERNET

Over 100,000 photographs of Britain can be viewed and purchased on the Frith web site. The web site also includes memories and reminiscences contributed by our customers, who have personal knowledge of localities and of the people and properties depicted in Frith photographs. If you wish to learn more about a specific town or village you may find these reminiscences fascinating to browse. Why not add your own comments if you think they would be of interest to others? See **www.francisfrith.com**

PLEASE HELP US BRING FRITH'S PHOTOGRAPHS TO LIFE

Our authors do their best to recount the history of the places they write about. They give insights into how particular towns and villages developed, they describe the architecture of streets and buildings, and they discuss the lives of famous people who lived there. But however knowledgeable our authors are, the story they tell is necessarily incomplete.

Frith's photographs are so much more than plain historical documents. They are living proofs of the flow of human life down the generations. They show real people at real moments in history; and each of those people is the son or daughter of someone, the brother or sister, aunt or uncle, grandfather or grandmother of someone else. All of them lived, worked and played in the streets depicted in Frith's photographs.

We would be grateful if you would give us your insights into the places shown in our photographs: the streets and buildings, the shops, businesses and industries. Post your memories of life in those streets on the Frith website: what it was like growing up there, who ran the local shop and what shopping was like years ago; if your workplace is shown tell us about your working day and what the building is used for now. Read other visitors' memories and reconnect with your shared local history and heritage. With your help more and more Frith photographs can be brought to life, and vital memories preserved for posterity, and for the benefit of historians in the future.

Wherever possible, we will try to include some of your comments in future editions of our books. Moreover, if you spot errors in dates, titles or other facts, please let us know, because our archive records are not always completely accurate—they rely on 140 years of human endeavour and hand-compiled records. You can email us using the contact form on the website.

Thank you!

For further information, trade, or author enquiries
please contact us at the address below:

**The Francis Frith Collection, Frith's Barn, Teffont,
Salisbury, Wiltshire, England SP3 5QP.**

Tel: +44 (0)1722 716 376 Fax: +44 (0)1722 716 881
e-mail: sales@francisfrith.co.uk **www.francisfrith.com**